nice!

i'm crushing it

belongs to: ------

Made in the USA
Monee, IL
04 August 2021

74896277R00066